WEALD and DOWNLAND COUNTRY

Painted by Wilfrid Ball R.E.
with drawings by Frederick L. Griggs R. A.

SALMON

Published by
J Salmon Limited
100 London Road, Sevenoaks,
Kent TN13 1BB

First edition 1995

Designed by the Salmon Studio

Copyright © 1995 J Salmon Limited

ISBN 1 898435 26 X

Printed in England by
J Salmon Limited, Tubs Hill Works
Sevenoaks, Kent

THE SUSSEX HILLS

Coloured Illustrations

THE CROSS, CHICHESTER

Chichester Harbour

AROUND CHICHESTER

To anyone who approaches this corner of Sussex by one or other of the magnificent routes across the Downs from Midhurst, Petworth or Pulborough, the landscape of the coastal flats may seem to present an anti-climax after a journey so satisfying in scenic interest. The visitor to the coast and countryside around Chichester must seek for its charm in ways other than the grandeur of the landscape. For, on most days, what pleasanter place can there be in which to spend lazy hours enjoying the local colour than around the shores and among the creeks of Chichester Harbour. At Dell Quay, Itchenor and Bosham you will find all the atmosphere of the sea and ships; muddy margins, noisy gulls and the colours and shapes of old quays and warehouses.

At Bosham, too, there is a link with the past, for, in addition to the old houses near the harbour, the ancient Saxon church by the village green greets the incoming ships. There can be no better approach to the city of Chichester than to arrive by sea, and land on the historic shore at Bosham. Even more secluded is West Wittering with its inn and old church; towards Selsey Bill the flat landscape is intersected by numerous dykes and the pebble beach seems but frail protection from the mighty sea.

The tall spire of Chichester Cathedral, 277 feet above the plain, serves as a landmark for miles around. From the Bell Tower one may survey the city; the four streets of the Roman plan dictated the site

Boxgrove from the south

of the highly decorated market cross erected in the fifteenth century. Apart from the wealth of interest in the cathedral itself there are numerous architectural treasures in the city and, behind the cathedral, is that peaceful retreat where lie the Bishops Palace and pleasant secluded gardens.

On the Sussex sea-plain additional interest is given by the backdrop of the Downs, and on those occasions when great cumulus clouds float across an intensive blue sky the effect can be superb. As for the villages they have retained their local character and there are splendid examples of ancient churches, such as the priory at Boxgrove.

ST. RICHARD'S WALK, CHICHESTER CATHEDRAL

THE VILLAGE POND, SINGLETON

THE WATERSIDE, BOSHAM

HERSTMONCEUX CASTLE

Court Lodge, Udimore

THE LEVELS AND 1066 COUNTRY

THE MARSHES AROUND Rye and Winchelsea, and the Pevensey Levels, represent two low-lying exposed areas where man has contested precariously with sea and river floods. In the 13th century the encroachment of the sea destroyed old Winchelsea, but later, after a period of prosperity as rival ports, both Rye and new Winchelsea, built by Edward I, were left high and dry by the retreat of the sea and the silt brought down by the Rother and the Brede. So now when one surveys the levels from the old Strand Gate of Winchelsea one faces a pastoral landscape where sheep now graze but once ships rode at anchor.

The historic significance of this area far exceeds its landscape interest. At Pevensey on a slight eminence the Romans established their great fortress of Anderida. Here too, on the shores of Pevensey Bay, Duke William landed his forces before he marched to Hastings. Today the grim walls of the castle give evidence of this thrilling and tragic past. Close by, yet altogether different, are the red-brick turrets and gatehouse of Herstmonceux Castle. In a secluded position, it is surrounded by a moat and graced with greensward courtyards and beautiful gardens.

The Refectory, Battle Abbey

At Battle one is on ground equally redolent with significance in the history of England. Standing in the Abbey grounds one can visualise the scene as it must have appeared when the Saxons occupied their position near what is now the terrace and the Normans were encamped between Telham Hill and Bodehurst Wood. They had approached that day from the direction of Hastings whose

THE SHORE, OLD HASTINGS

castle ruins recall the town's history as the fist Norman stronghold. Hastings and St. Leonards have managed to combine what remains of the characteristic little fishing town with an early Victorian seaside resort.

Rye is fortunate in its spectacular site which has necessitated the compactly built streets clustered around the church. The

Westham

picturesque quality of Watchbell Street and Mermaid Street, the ancient Mermaid Inn, the medieval gates, the church and the Ypres Tower, the mill and quayside all create an atmosphere of antiquity. Whether viewed from the marshes when its silhouette is outlined against the setting sun, or examined in detail within the encircling walls, this little town is as beautiful a place as any on the Channel coast.

THE MERMAID INN, RYE

BATTLE ABBEY GATEWAY

BODIAM CASTLE

PEVENSEY CASTLE

WINCHELSEA

THE BARBICAN, LEWES CASTLE

Chanctonbury Ring

THE SOUTH DOWNS

SUSSEX MAY ENVY those more favoured counties which possess magnificent cliffs and good coastal walks where the visitor, as in Devon and Cornwall, can always maintain close contact with the sea; but there is equal charm and variety in the landscape to be enjoyed by following the tops of the Downs from Hampshire to their dramatic climax at Beachy Head. Moreover at every stage there are those characteristic little towns and villages which lie so invitingly snug under the shadow of the hills. In the west the hills cut the line of old Stane Street near Bignor, where the track-way descends to the village and the remains of its Roman villa.

One of the best known viewpoints in West Sussex is at the top of Bury Hill looking north-east towards Amberley. Below, the Arun is crossed by Houghton Bridge and the little community of chalk and flint cottages at Amberley clusters round the Norman church. The view embraces both weald and downland and the green parkland

and woods of Parham House. In contrast to the well-wooded hills between the Arun and Hampshire, the Downs here present their well-rounded forms, bare of trees, and the noble silhouette of Chanctonbury Ring dominates the country for miles around. From the tree-crowned summit, one can gaze far across the Weald, with its hamlets and farmhouses appearing like islands in a green sea of pastures and woods; to the north the horizon is the distant Forest

Sompting Church

ridge and southwards the blue outline of Cissbury Ring stands out with the sea at Worthing beyond. Here the Saxon church of Sompting nestles beneath the slopes.

From Steyning to Lewes long fingers of chalk stretch out to the sea plain and below the crest are the Saxon settlements at Edburton, Fulking and Poynings. At Steyning it seems incredible that the town was among the largest in England at the time of the Domesday Book, when the Adur was navigable to Bramber Castle.

Beyond Devils Dyke, a popular place for visitors from Brighton seeking the Downland air, appear the old windmills at Clayton and

BURY FROM THE ARUN

COTTAGES AT GLYNDE

MALLING MILL

THE STAR INN, ALFRISTON

BEACHY HEAD

PULBOROUGH CHURCH

Cowdray Ruins, Midhurst

THE ARUN AND WESTERN ROTHER

THE RIVER ARUN is the longest and perhaps the most beautiful river in the county. It rises near Selborne in Hampshire and from its source to its junction with the River Avon near Loxwood it is known as the Western Rother.

In the variety of its scenery, in the number of its ancient bridges, and in the characteristic villages on its banks, the Rother is unsurpassed. All the way from Durford to Pulborough it is an entrancing stream. At Midhurst it sweeps round the town to enhance the beauty of Cowdray House and its gracious park; not far distant the little town of Petworth huddles close to the high stone walls of Petworth House as if for protection.

The Rother is fortunately accessible at very frequent intervals and there are numerous crossings from which to gaze into its clear waters. There are fine bridges at Iping and Stedham and who has not hung over the three stone arches of sixteenth century Fittleworth Bridge; but the best of all is at Stopham, with its seven sturdy arches carrying the main Pulborough to Petworth road. Here the Arun mingles with tidal waters, and so on past Pulborough and Amberley, until it passes with great loops through the Downland gap to Arundel.

There is surely no more dramatic view than that of Arundel, standing proudly with its grey battlements on a bluff overlooking the Arun Valley, and intimately connected with the little feudal town over which it keeps watch. Since the site was first occupied by

Stopham Bridge

the Saxons and subsequently fortified by Roger de Montgomery the castle has had a thrilling history of siege and change of ownership, with the result that there is little of the original fortress extant.

Downstream with ever-widening channel, the river takes its serpentine course through the wet, bare pastures of the coastal plain to the diminutive harbour at Littlehampton.

SOUTH POND, MIDHURST

THE SWAN INN, FITTLEWORTH

ARUNDEL CASTLE

THE PANTILES, TUNBRIDGE WELLS

Ashdown Forest from East Grinstead

AROUND ASHDOWN FOREST

APART FROM THE South Downs, the outstanding feature of the Sussex landscape is the Forest country, consisting of a range of wooded hills embracing Ashdown Forest, all that remains of that great forest belt which once stretched into Hampshire and Kent. From Crowborough Beacon extends a prospect of the Weald and Downs and to the west a great area of forest and heath.

In order to appreciate the real glory of Ashdown one must traverse the Forest on foot from Crowborough to Wych Cross, for then you can explore the bracken and heathland around Camp Hill and the woodlands of oak, ash and other native trees in the series of valleys to the east and west of the ridge. The stranger may not realise that the Camp

Hill heights were also once well covered with timber before it was cleared to provide fuel for the flourishing local iron foundries.

Hereabouts are to be seen some of the most delightful villages of Sussex, although they are few and far apart. At Frant the pretty cottages and green welcome the traveller from Tunbridge Wells. The villages of Withyham and Hartfield are among the best in Sussex and both are possessed of picturesque old inns. Southwards one can strike out to the Wealden country around Uckfield and the villages of Maresfield, Buxted and Framfield.

Framfield

On the Forest's western fringes are Wych Cross and West Hoathly with its fine church and old manor house. From here extends a belt of well-wooded country, all that remains of the old St. Leonards Forest, watered by the headwaters of the Ouse and the Medway. Its northerly outpost is East Grinstead, a pleasant place with the raised sidewalks and old houses of the High Street, and the church and Sackville College.

CROWBOROUGH HEATH

THE INN, HARTFIELD

HIGH STREET, EAST GRINSTEAD

COTTAGES AT SLINFOLD

The Causeway, Horsham

AROUND THE WEALD

FOR THE MOST part the Weald of Sussex is agricultural and a complex network of lanes still represents the only means of communication between many village settlements which owe their origins to forest clearings or the presence of ironstone. Whence it abuts the sandy hills of Surrey in the west, the woodland and pasture landscape stretches in a belt across the middle of the county.

Among the Wealden towns, Lindfield with its pond is very picturesque. From the churchyard of neighbouring Cuckfield there is a wonderful view of the distant Downs and at Horsham, the 'capital' of the western Weald, the peaceful causeway leading up to the tall-spired church is lined with trees and old houses.

For picturesque villages the Weald is well blest with delights; Mayfield with its many houses of architectural interest, the charming weather-boarded mill at Chailey, and Wisborough and Kirdford in the west with their expansive greenswards, to name but a few.

A WEALDEN FARMSTEAD

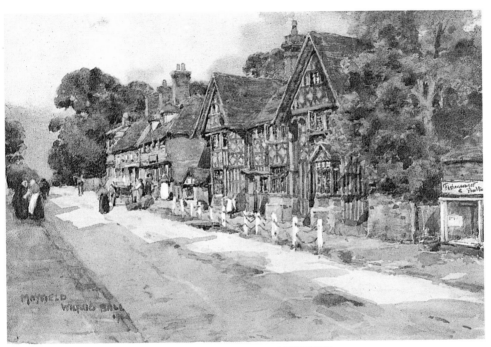

THE MIDDLE HOUSE, MAYFIELD

CUCKFIELD CHURCH